PURPOS

TEEN & YOUNG ADULT WORKBOOK

Priscilla Allman

PURPOSE OF Heart

FAMILY BIBLE STUDY COLLECTION

A Family Bible Study

Purpose of Heart roars into action, a dynamic Family Bible Study focused on Daniel. Over nine sessions, dive deep into God's Word, extracting treasures through engaging lessons, reflection, and interactive activities. Join the action, learn, have a blast, and strengthen family bonds!
ISBN: 979-8-9899839-4-0

The Ultimate Workbook for Little Ones (2-6 years)! Bursting with carefully selected, action-packed activities synced with each Purpose of Heart session on Daniel. Join the family quest, explore God's Word, and uncover treasures through dynamic lessons, reflections, and exciting activities. Get ready for a whirlwind of learning, fun, and strengthened family bonds!
ISBN: 979-8-9899839-0-2

CHILD WORKBOOK

The Ultimate Workbook for Kids (7-13 years)! Loaded with carefully chosen, high-energy activities perfectly synced with each Purpose of Heart session on Daniel. Unite with your family, dive into God's Word and extract treasures through engaging lessons, reflections, and fun-filled activities. Gear up for an adventure of learning, fun, and strengthened family bonds!
ISBN: 979-8-9899839-1-9

Unveiling the Teen & Young Adult's Workbook - an action packed guide for ages 14-21+! Brimming with carefully chosen, dynamic activities perfectly synced with each session in Purpose of Heart, a Family Bible Study on Daniel. Join the adventure, unite with your family, explore God's Word, and unearth treasures through engaging sessions. Dive into lessons, reflections, and high-energy activities for an impactful journey of learning, enjoyment, and strengthened family bonds!
ISBN: 979-8-9899839-2-6

Parent WorkBook

Bursting with carefully chosen, engaging activities that sync seamlessly with each session in the main study. Purpose of Heart, a Family Bible Study on Daniel invites families to actively learn, glean treasures, and strengthen bonds through dynamic lessons and reflective activities. Elevate your family experience with this action-packed workbook!
ISBN: 979-8-9899839-3-3

Your Free Gift!

www.mepublishing.co/freebies

To connect with Priscilla for more resources and the keepsake family treasure box to accompany the study go to

www.mepublishing.co

ISBN: 979-8-9899839-2-6

About the Author

Priscilla Allman is the esteemed President and Founder of Bridges to Wholeness Education Group and the M & E Institute for Mentorship and Academic Excellence. She holds a Bachelor of Arts in Music from The College of New Jersey and is currently pursuing her Doctor of Medicine at Rutgers New Jersey Medical School.

With a distinguished background as a professional violinist and violist, Priscilla's global travels included imparting musical knowledge to students of diverse age groups, utilizing music as a powerful catalyst for social change. Her expertise extends to being a sought-after speaker and mentor, where she has effectively leveraged her platforms to serve underserved populations by providing valuable resources, thereby accelerating their growth and potential.

Beyond her role as a Christian author, Priscilla is a published poet and researcher with diverse projects spanning Music, Neurology, Emergency Medicine, Clinical Dermatology, and Maternal and Fetal Mortality.

A fervent advocate for education, Priscilla perceives it as the bridge to connection. Her overarching goals involve advancing wealth and wellness through education in a manner that is both engaging and God-honoring. She is driven to positively impact lives, drawing inspiration from the support she has received throughout her own journey.

In addition to her leadership roles, Priscilla is an accomplished performance violinist, violist, and educator. As a career-changer and committed future physician, she brings a unique blend of skills to her endeavors, with a particular focus on addressing health inequities. Her entrepreneurial spirit, coupled with extensive performance and teaching experience, underscores her commitment to utilizing all of her talents as a vehicle for social change and innovation.

Priscilla has a dedicated history of serving in various capacities, aligning with her passion for education and community service. Her multifaceted contributions, paired with her commitment to excellence, exemplify her as a leader in both the educational and medical spheres.

Priscilla Allman

Dedicated to my Grandmother

Frances L. Taitt

Deuteronomy 31:13 "and that their children, who have not known it, may hear and learn to fear the Lord your God as long as you live in the land which you cross the Jordan to possess."

To my cherished "Old Lady," a title filled with love and admiration. With the words of Deuteronomy 31:13, you, my 100-year-old grandma, imparted a timeless charge - that my children, yet unknown, may learn to fear the Lord.

On that significant day, you not only shared a verse but instilled a legacy. From leading me to Christ to teaching me the power of prayer, your influence shaped my journey. Your love for cooking, a delicious thread woven into the fabric of our family.

Throughout my life, I witnessed your resilience, endurance, and the radiant joy you bring to others, even in your golden years. Your life's touch has left indelible imprints scattered far and wide. Your fingerprints of love and legacy are scattered all around, touching countless lives.

As I walk the journey of guiding and nurturing the next generation, I will carry your charge close to my heart. May I reflect even a fraction of the remarkable woman you are. Your life, a testament to faith, love, and enduring joy, inspires me every day. I pray I make you proud, aiming to honor the incredible legacy you've gifted me.

With Love and Admiration
Your Favorite,
Poopsie

Contents

Session 1	11
Between Sessions 1	15
Session 2	23
Between Sessions 2	29
Session 3	39
Between Sessions 3	45
Session 4	53
Between Sessions 4	59
Session 5	65
Between Sessions 5	75
Session 6	79
Between Sessions 6	87

Session 7 93
Between Sessions 7 101
Session 8 107
Between Sessions 8 115
Session 9 121
How to be Saved 130

In the world today, there are so many things to do, everything is so fast paced, we all have our goals and ambitions, the legitimate things we work towards. Sometimes it is so easy to get bogged down, to just try to get by and get through. I've done that, hit the wall a few times, and wondered what was wrong. Thinking that I'm trying to do this, that, and the other, but still not making the progress I thought I would, coming up against many barriers and hindrances to the life I'm truly trying to live.

PURPOSE OF HEART is like a steering wheel, it directs and controls, enabling one to stay the course. Life is hard, and sometimes it surprises me how hard it can be. As I drive through life there are detours, bumps, roadkill, fallen trees and other random mishaps along the way. While it may not always go to plan, and there's a hiccup along the journey, there's so much beauty as well!

My hope is that through this book we together are encouraged to first have the right destination in view, to keep steering in that direction, and to recognize beauty along the way. My desire is that every family is whole and living how God intends. That there is this focus and determination starting with the parents down to the littlest ones. That you get clarity from the Lord about the direction He is leading your family, and that ultimately we all bring glory to Him.

No more are we settling for getting halfway there. No more are we "just good enough." No more are we leaving people behind, or your kids getting out at a different stop. We are all getting there to the finish line, together! As a family! No ifs, ands, or buts. We will have *PURPOSE OF HEART!*

Join me as we look at Daniel's example, how from a young age, he chose to steer his car in one direction and he didn't give up. He stayed the course through being captive, thrown in a lion's den, accused and more. **He stayed focused and God delivered him, time and time again.**

I don't know who you are, or where you've been or what you're going through, but I want to encourage you, as I do myself, that the same God that kept Daniel, will keep you and your family.

It may look horrible now, everything may be in flames and insane. But like Daniel, we will have confidence in God that He will work it out and enable us to do His will in living for Him. With His help, we are going to pick up where we are, deal with the baggage, leave the past behind, and get back on course.

I may never meet you, but I hope in some small way that you win, that your family wins and that you all succeed as you all stay focused on Him. So whether you've gotten off track, or have never been on track, let's work together to get our families back on track.

let's have Purpose of Heart!

DANIEL 1:8

But Daniel ***PURPOSED IN HIS HEART*** *that he would not defile himself with the portion of the king's meat, nor with the wine which he drank; therefore he requested of the prince of the eunuchs that he might not defile himself.*

SESSION 1

HEZEKIAH WAS RELIEVED THAT HIS DECISION WOULDN'T AFFECT HIM.

What do you think a better response could be?

HEZEKIAH'S RESPONSE IS, THE OPPOSITE OF REPENTANCE AND ACCOUNTABILITY

What are some ways this week that you can be accountable?

Do you think something could have changed if Hezekiah had a different response?

Are there behaviors you need to examine, and be mindful of the long-term consequences?

LARI- What one thing can you learn and apply this week?

I learned ______________________________

I will apply it by ______________________________

Review/Improve ______________________________

TREASURE- What one thing struck you as significant, important, or interesting? Use the "Treasures" provided

BETWEEN SESSION WORKBOOK

The preacher's dad made a life choice that impacted future generations. Even though he initially faced opposition from his wife, he was committed to his decision to live for Christ, and eventually, his family was saved. It's crazy to think that his decision and commitment to follow through were so important! Sit back and dream with me for a moment... Think about yourself 5 years from now.

What does your life look like? What are you doing? Where do you go to school, and what hobbies, adventures, or jobs do you have?

____

____

Now think about your choices. Are they aligned with where you want to go?

____

____

For instance, (I know this is not you; I'm just exaggerating here for emphasis), let's say you dream of going to an Ivy League College, but you are getting straight F's because you don't take the time to study. You could start studying and get a tutor to get better grades, which would align you better with your dream.

WHILE EDUCATION, TRAVEL, JOBS, AND LIVING LIFE ARE IMPORTANT, THE MOST IMPORTANT CHOICE YOU CAN MAKE IS TO LIVE FOR CHRIST!

Are the shows or movies you watch helping you live a Godly life?

Is the music you listen to glorifying God? How about your friends?

Do they encourage you to do things that you know are wrong?

Do you obey and honor your parents as it says in Ephesians 6:1-3?

How can you better align your life choices to enable you to follow Christ better?

WE WILL LEARN THAT DANIEL WAS A "YOUNG MAN," BUT HIS CHOICES WERE SIGNIFICANT, AND YOURS ARE TOO. DON'T THINK THAT FOR ONE SECOND YOU'RE NOT IMPORTANT AND YOU CAN'T MAKE A DIFFERENCE.

It says in **EPHESIANS 2:10** that "We are His masterpiece..." Now a masterpiece is not junk; it's not leftovers, it's valuable, treasured, significant. Don't let anyone, the devil and yourself included, deceive you into thinking that whatever you're doing or thinking "doesn't really matter, it won't really make a difference."

In JOHN 6:9-14 we see the story of the boy with 5 loaves and 2 fish. It was a small meal in his hands, but he made a decision and spoke up. He gave all that he had, and in the hands of Jesus, it was multiplied to feed over 5,000 people to the point that they were filled and had leftovers!!! My dear friend, you can make a decision and give what you have to the Lord, and in His hands, He will make it significant!

HOW ARE YOU COMING ALONG WITH YOUR LARI?

SESSION 2

CONSIDER THESE VERSES AS YOU GO THROUGH THE FOLLOWING QUESTIONS:

1 John 2:16-17, Proverbs 20:11, and 1 Thessalonians 2:7-8,11-12

What is your name, and what does it mean?

Why is your name important?

Why do you think they changed the four boys' names?

Do you have pressures at school or with your friends to do or learn things you know are wrong?

How does that make you feel?

Is there something you can do about it?

Is there something you need help with?

THEY LOOKED FOR THOSE WHO WERE SMART, TALENTED, AND GOOD-LOOKING TO USE FOR THEIR OWN PURPOSES.

Are there certain things about your life, talents, gifts, and looks that you are using for the world's benefit and not for Christ's?

What do you think is the significance of them looking for those characteristics?

What do you think is the significance of changed names?

What can you do to guard against being used in such a way?

LARI- What one thing can you learn and apply this week?

I learned ______________________________

I will apply it by ______________________________

Review/Improve______________________________

TREASURE- What one thing struck you as significant, important, or interesting? Use the "Treasures" provided

BETWEEN SESSION WORKBOOK

THE KING OF BABYLON, TOOK YOUNG MEN OF A CERTAIN CALIBER WITH CERTAIN CHARACTERISTICS.

What were some of them, and how do they relate to you?

In school or at work this week, how can you better show that you are a child of God, and take on His name?

What choices are you making now that you should make differently?

HOW ARE YOU COMING ALONG WITH YOUR LARI?

Names and identity are important for youths, but they are important for parents and older ones as well, without a clear view of who we are in Christ, we can be acting in a way not according to our name!

God says you are His! He calls us by name Isaiah 43:1-2, what an awesome thought to know that we are precious, sought after, and identified by an all loving, all powerful God! We learned in the family devotional that He gives us a new nature and makes us His children, through the gift of Jesus on the cross we now are in the family of God!

NEW IDENTITY!

There are so many voices out there, telling you who you are, or who you should be, but let's look to the ultimate Authority and see what He has to say about who we are!

Ephesians 2:10 "For we are His masterpiece. He has created us anew in Christ Jesus, so we can do the good things He planned for us long ago." (NLT)

DID YOU GET THAT, YOU ARE A MASTERPIECE!

Let that sink in!

More precious to God the Father than all the most priceless artworks that have ever been or will ever be created!

I want to share my most favorite verses with you. Isaiah 43:1-5a

"But now, thus says the Lord, who created you, O Jacob, And He who formed you, O Israel: "Fear not, for I have redeemed you; I have called you by your name; You are Mine. When you pass through the waters, I will be with you; And through the rivers, they shall not overflow you. When you walk through the fire, you shall not be burned, nor shall the flame scorch you. For I am the Lord your God, The Holy One of Israel, your Savior; I gave Egypt for your ransom, Ethiopia and Seba in your place. Since you were precious in My sight, and because I love you, you have been honored; therefore I will give men for you, And people for your life. Fear not for I am with you..."

GOD SAYS YOU ARE HIS! HE CALLS US BY NAME!

What security, what a promise!
How significant, cared for and loved you are!
The God of the universe is always with you,
He formed you, He preserves you,
He will give anything for you including His Son Jesus to die in your place so that you can have a relationship with Him!
He is with you and loves you perfectly!
The God of ALL says you are significant!
So don't ever let anyone, the devil, or even yourself tell you you are insignificant!
Characterize yourself by His labels ONLY!
Take His name!

Write down some affirmations for yourself aligned with who God says you are!

AFFIRMATIONS

SCRIPTURE READING CHALLENGE

I READ MY BIBLE TODAY:

Day 1	Day 2	Day 3	Day 4	Day 5	Day 6	Day 7

I PRAYED TODAY:

Day 1	Day 2	Day 3	Day 4	Day 5	Day 6	Day 7

SESSION 3

If you're honest with yourself, do you dabble in the king's delicacies?

Why or why not?

Do you think that it even matters if you do or don't?

Do you think your friends are a good influence?

Why or why not?

Are you a good influence?

What are you consuming?

Have you purposed in your heart who you're going to serve?

LARI- What one thing can you learn and apply this week?

I learned ______________________________

I will apply it by ______________________________

Review/Improve______________________________

TREASURE- What one thing struck you as significant, important, or interesting? Use the "Treasures" provided

BETWEEN SESSION WORKBOOK

If there are some areas where you could be dieting better personally, take a moment to prayerfully bring them before the Lord and make changes where necessary. Ask the Lord for guidance on how to make these changes!

- **CHOICE**

- **CHANGE**

Do I watch, listen to, or read things that I know I shouldn't be?

Do I engage in activities, jokes, etc., that I know are not honoring the Lord?

Am I hiding something that I know my parents and, most importantly, God won't approve of?

Do I have good friends?

Do they encourage me spiritually, like to read or pray?

Do we pray together?

By my choices in school or at work, can others see I belong to Christ?

AM I EATING VEGGIES AMIDST THE KING'S DELICACIES?

____

____

Does something in the world tempt me, that just looks like it would be "sooooooo tasty?" If so, what?

____

____

Is it good for me and God-honoring? If not, do I believe that God will help me resist and give me a blessing?

____

____

Do my friends know I'm a Christian, or do I act so much like them that no one would know the difference?

____

____

Daniel and his friends' actions showed that they were set apart! Do people know what team you're on?

If someone made a movie of your life, and strangers worldwide watched it, what would people think about you?

Would they even guess that you're a Christian?

MOVIE PLOT TWIST!

If the movie is not going in the most positive direction now, can you introduce a "plot-twist" by God's help? Outline it now below!

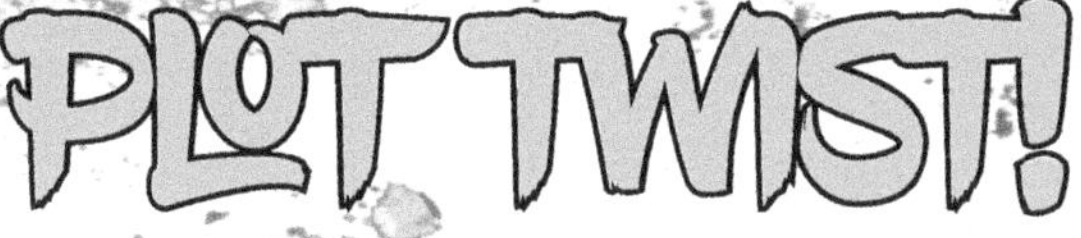

Below outline the scene that will change the events of the main characters life....
. . . . . A N D ACTION!
What was the change?

SCENE 1	SCENE 2

HOW ARE YOU COMING ALONG WITH YOUR LARI?

SESSION 4

How do you solve problems?

What was the last crisis you had?

How did your emotions feel? Are there ways that you can better manage next time?

Let's take a step back and outline Daniel's response to crisis, does yours look similar?

VERSE 15	Daniel finds out what the urgent matter is.
VERSE 16	Presents a request.
VERSES 17-18	He presents it to his Godly, like-minded friends (companions, church family), and they go before the Lord together (I under stand all matters may not be shareable with everyone, use discretion).
VERSE 19	Once an answer was received from God, Daniel praises (before the matter was even fixed, before the king)
VERSE 28	Daniel points the king to God.
VERSE 30	Daniel had a humble spirit and was not puffed up because he "saved himself and the other wise men."

WHILE EVERY PROBLEM YOU MAY NOT SHARE WITH OTHERS, THE OVERALL STRUCTURE IS IMPORTANT: WHEN FACED WITH A CRISIS

1. **Get further information/clarity if possible**
2. **Pray (Seek the Lord's revelation, by yourself or in community (how blessed to have prayer partners and Godly friendships!)**
3. **Praise**
4. **Stay humble**

What are your prayer habits? Is there someone whom you partner in prayer with to pray not just for yourself and your family but for issues in your community, other families, and the world?

LARI- What one thing can you learn and apply this week?

I learned ______________________________

I will apply it by ______________________________

Review/Improve______________________________

TREASURE- What one thing struck you as significant, important, or interesting? Use the "Treasures" provided

BETWEEN SESSION WORKBOOK

TAKE SOME TIME TO FOCUS ON YOUR PRAYER LIFE AND HEALTH BETWEEN SESSIONS AND ALSO FOCUS ON IMMEDIATELY PRAISING GOD AFTER BLESSINGS!

Daniel had a lot to fear; his life was in danger!
How can you better take your cares, anxieties, and worries to Jesus?
Is there something bothering you?
Is there something you are afraid of?

TELL JESUS, YOUR LOVING FATHER, ABOUT IT!

PRAYER JOURNAL

REQUEST	WHEN I ASKED (DATE)	WHEN GOD ANSWERED (DATE)

WHAT A FRIEND WE HAVE IN JESUS

What a Friend we have in Jesus, all our sins and griefs to bear!

What a privilege to carry everything to God in prayer!

O What peace we often forfeit, O what needless pain we bear,

All because we do not carry everything to God in prayer.

Joseph M. Scriven

HOW ARE YOU COMING ALONG WITH YOUR LARI?

SESSION 5

TAKE THIS TIME TO TAKE ANYTHING THAT YOU ARE GOING THROUGH, ANY TRIAL, HEARTACHE OR PAIN AND GIVE IT TO JESUS. JOURNAL A LITTLE BIT ON THE PAGES TO FOLLOW AFTER READING THROUGH THE NEXT FEW PSALMS 23, 40, 91

PSALM 23

The Lord is my shepherd;
I shall not want.
He makes me to lie down in green pastures;
He leads me beside the still waters.
He restores my soul;
He leads me in the paths of righteousness
For His name's sake.

Yea, though I walk through the valley of the shadow of death,
I will fear no evil;
For You are with me;
Your rod and Your staff, they comfort me.

You prepare a table before me in the presence of my enemies;
You anoint my head with oil;
My cup runs over.
Surely goodness and mercy shall follow me
All the days of my life;
And I will dwell in the house of the Lord
Forever.

PSALM 40

I waited patiently for the Lord;
And He inclined to me,
And heard my cry.
He also brought me up out of a horrible pit,
Out of the miry clay,
And set my feet upon a rock,
And established my steps.
He has put a new song in my mouth—
Praise to our God;
Many will see it and fear,
And will trust in the Lord.

Blessed is that man who makes the Lord his trust,
And does not respect the proud, nor such as turn aside to lies.
Many, O Lord my God, are Your wonderful works
Which You have done;
And Your thoughts toward us
Cannot be recounted to You in order;
If I would declare and speak of them,
They are more than can be numbered.

Sacrifice and offering You did not desire;
My ears You have opened.
Burnt offering and sin offering You did not require.
Then I said, "Behold, I come;
In the scroll of the book it is written of me.
I delight to do Your will, O my God,
And Your law is within my heart."

I have proclaimed the good news of righteousness
In the great assembly;
Indeed, I do not restrain my lips,
O Lord, You Yourself know.
I have not hidden Your righteousness within my heart;
I have declared Your faithfulness and Your salvation;
I have not concealed Your loving kindness and Your truth
From the great assembly.

Do not withhold Your tender mercies from me, O Lord;
Let Your loving kindness and Your truth continually preserve me.
For innumerable evils have surrounded me;
My iniquities have overtaken me, so that I am not able to look up;
They are more than the hairs of my head;
Therefore my heart fails me.

Be pleased, O Lord, to deliver me;
O Lord, make haste to help me!
Let them be ashamed and brought to mutual confusion
Who seek to destroy my life;
Let them be driven backward and brought to dishonor
Who wish me evil.
Let them be confounded because of their shame,
Who say to me, "Aha, aha!"

Let all those who seek You rejoice and be glad in You;
Let such as love Your salvation say continually,
"The Lord be magnified!"
But I am poor and needy;
Yet the Lord thinks upon me.
You are my help and my deliverer;
Do not delay, O my God.

PSALM 91

He who dwells in the secret place of the Most High
Shall abide under the shadow of the Almighty.
I will say of the Lord, "He is my refuge and my fortress;
My God, in Him I will trust."

Surely He shall deliver you from the snare of the fowler
And from the perilous pestilence.
He shall cover you with His feathers,
And under His wings you shall take refuge;
His truth shall be your shield and buckler.
You shall not be afraid of the terror by night,
Nor of the arrow that flies by day,
Nor of the pestilence that walks in darkness,
Nor of the destruction that lays waste at noonday.

A thousand may fall at your side,
And ten thousand at your right hand;
But it shall not come near you.
Only with your eyes shall you look,
And see the reward of the wicked.

Because you have made the Lord, who is my refuge,
Even the Most High, your dwelling place,
No evil shall befall you,
Nor shall any plague come near your dwelling;
For He shall give His angels charge over you,
To keep you in all your ways.
In their hands they shall bear you up,
Lest you dash your foot against a stone.
You shall tread upon the lion and the cobra,
The young lion and the serpent you shall trample underfoot.

"Because he has set his love upon Me, therefore I will deliver him;
I will set him on high, because he has known My name.
He shall call upon Me, and I will answer him;
I will be with him in trouble;
I will deliver him and honor him.
With long life I will satisfy him,
And show him My salvation."

JOURNAL PAGES

LARI- What one thing can you learn and apply this week?

I learned ____

I will apply it by ____

Review/Improve____

TREASURE- What one thing struck you as significant, important, or interesting? Use the "Treasures" provided

BETWEEN SESSION WORKBOOK

WRITE A PSALM OR POEM SHOWING HOW YOU SEE GOD IN YOUR CIRCUMSTANCE!
USE THE PSALMS 23, 40, AND 91 FOR REFERENCE

SESSION 6

Being excellent, doing well in school, work, sports and in general is a good thing. But it can become a bad thing when it turns over into pride. It is so easy to have confidence in your abilities, in your youth, beauty, handsomeness, intelligence, strength, and health. But as we saw in our story, once we make the switch into pride, into thinking we are invincible and can do it all without God, that's where we run into trouble.

Are you willing to ask God where in your life are areas of pride?

____

____

And are you willing to submit those to Him, acknowledging that in Him we move and have our being, that He gives you breath and allows you to excel and thrive?

____

____

What is the difference between taking pride in what you do and being prideful?

____

____

Is there any difference?

What does ***Proverbs 16:18-19*** mean to you?

How is it a warning about some area in your life?

How can you apply these verses to your life?

What does ***Ephesians 6:1-2*** state? How can you better live out these verses in your life?

NEBUCHADNEZZAR'S ATTITUDE EXHIBITED HIS PRIDE. HE USED HIS POSITION AS KING TO GET THE PEOPLE HE WAS IN CHARGE OVER TO DO HIS BIDDING, AND HE PLACED HIMSELF IN A POSITION THAT ONLY GOD SHOULD HAVE.

LARI- What one thing can you learn and apply this week?

I learned ____

I will apply it by ____________________________________

Review/Improve______________________________________

TREASURE- What one thing struck you as significant, important, or interesting?
Use the "Treasures" provided

BETWEEN SESSION WORKBOOK

If I work, babysit, or have some other form of leadership, do I abuse it and let it get to my head, or am I a gracious boss, host, babysitter, etc?

Do I work with others well, or is it all about how things can benefit me?

What do you think a leader is?

What do you think a follower is?

What makes a good leader?

What makes a good follower?

Am I a leader or a follower?

If I am a leader, do I lead well?

Where can I improve?

If I am a follower, am I following the right things?

Do I make good decisions on who to follow?

Am I an example of Christ at school and at play?

If I make a mistake, do I learn from it, or do I keep doing the wrong thing over and over again?

If I do, why? Is there something I can do to change it?

SELF-ASSESSMENT

THINGS I NEED TO IMPROVE. . .

HOW ARE YOU COMING ALONG WITH YOUR LARI?

SESSION 7

Have you ever been unjustly targeted?

What was your response?

What could be your future response if you may not have responded correctly?

ALTHOUGH DANIEL HAD A TRIAL BECAUSE OF AN EVIL PLOT AGAINST HIM, GOD WAS WITH HIM.

How does this encourage you to do the right thing and stay faithful to God despite difficulties?

READ DANIEL 6:22 FOR ENCOURAGEMENT.

Daniel 6:3 **mentions Daniel's "excellent spirit" that caused the king to ponder setting him over the whole realm.** ***Daniel 6:4*** **states, "So the**

governors and satraps sought to find some charge against Daniel concerning the kingdom; but they could find no charge or fault, because he was faithful; nor was there any error or fault found in him."

LET'S TAKE SOME TIME TO SELF-REFLECT AND ANSWER THESE QUESTIONS PRAYERFULLY BEFORE THE LORD.

How is my spirit? ______________________________

Would others say I have an excellent spirit? ______________________________

____

What would my friends, work/colleagues say about my spirit? ______________________________

Would they say the same things, or would they differ and why? ______________________________

Am I one person in a certain group and different in another? If yes, why? ______________________________

____

Am I faithful? Do I do my work, responsibilities, etc., as unto the Lord? Do I have a spirit of excellence? ______________________________

____

What steps can I take to be more excellent? ______________________________

____

____

We sometimes want our parents to trust us, to go certain places, or to have a driver's license/car without recognizing that we may have some habits that make them apprehensive about giving us that privilege. For example, you could want to go with a friend on a trip, but every time your parents let you go out, you come home waaaaaayyyyy after curfew, or you are never where you say you'll be.

What are some ways that you can correct this behavior to increase trust?

____

____

____

OFTEN, WE WANT GOD TO BLESS US WITH MORE WITHOUT BEING FAITHFUL TO WHAT IS ALREADY GIVEN.

How can you better steward what He has given you today?

____

 ____

LARI- What one thing can you learn and apply this week?

I learned ______________________________

I will apply it by ______________________________

Review/Improve______________________________

TREASURE- What one thing struck you as significant, important, or interesting?
Use the "Treasures" provided

BETWEEN SESSION WORKBOOK

Do we truly trust/believe God in the circumstances, or do we try and manipulate things to benefit us?

____

____

DANIEL SHOWED STEADFASTNESS IN PRAYER AND, THROUGH THAT STEADFASTNESS, SHOWED GOD'S POWER.

How is your prayer life? ______________________________

____

Do you talk to God at all? ______________________________

How can you increase it? ______________________________

Does it need to be reinvigorated? ______________________

What steps can you take today to be more consistent in prayer? __________

____

Previously, we had a prayer exercise; how is that journal going?

____

____

How can we be more faithful in prayer this week? Who do you pray for?

____

____

Is there any trial/circumstance that you need to depend on God for deliverance from?

____

____

SPEND SOME TIME IN PRAYER, ASKING HIM TO INTERCEDE ON YOUR BEHALF!

Do you pray for our leaders? ________________________________

Why______________________Why not____________________

____

Will you start?____

____

Do you consistently pray for others/friends/family and intercede on their behalf for God to make a way for them?

____

____

HOW ARE YOU COMING ALONG WITH YOUR LARI?

SESSION 8

CONSIDER THESE VERSES AS YOU GO THROUGH THE FOLLOWING QUESTIONS: PHILIPPIANS 4:6-7, JAMES 4:3, AND 1 PETER 5:7

Does it sometimes seem like you're praying and asking God for something and it seems like there is no answer?

It is so easy in those times to get discouraged. What are some practical steps that you can take to strengthen yourself when you are feeling weary in well doing?

SOME EXAMPLES ARE BELOW AND YOU CAN ADD TO THEM:

Sing/worship session, take a walk outside and spend time in nature in awe of all He has created, listen to a sermon, take a nap, eat a snack, write out a poem, set a timer and write down everything you are grateful for in one minute...

Therefore we also, since we are surrounded by so great a cloud of witnesses, let us lay aside every weight, and the sin which so easily ensnares us, and let us run with endurance the race that is set before us.

Hebrews 12:1

AS YOU GO THROUGH THE WEEK, START TO MEMORIZE HEBREWS 12:1

LARI- What one thing can you learn and apply this week?

I learned ______________________________

I will apply it by ______________________________

Review/Improve______________________________

TREASURE- What one thing struck you as significant, important, or interesting? Use the "Treasures" provided

BETWEEN SESSION WORKBOOK

What are some practical ways that you can run this race better with endurance?

First, are you running the race?

Have you slowed down, taken a detour, or run in the opposite direction?

Assess where you are; how can you better run?

Where can you improve?

What encouragement can you give your friends and younger siblings to run better?

How can you better align yourself under God's rule?

____

____

CONTINUE TO MEMORIZE HEBREWS 12:1

Therefore we also, since we are surrounded by so great a cloud of witnesses, let us lay aside every weight, and the sin which so easily ensnares us, and let us run with endurance the race that is set before us.

Hebrews 12:1

HOW ARE YOU COMING ALONG WITH YOUR LARI?

SESSION 9

CHARACTERISTICS' OF GOD

HIS ATTRIBUTES AS RELATED TO DANIEL

SESSION 1	
SESSION 2	
SESSION 3	
SESSION 4	
SESSION 5	
SESSION 6	
SESSION 7	
SESSION 8	

TREASURES

Session 1	
Session 2	
Session 3	
Session 4	
Session 5	
Session 6	
Session 7	
Session 8	

Session 1

L	
A	
R	
I	

Session 2

L	
A	
R	
I	

Session 3

L	
A	
R	
I	

Session 4	
L	
A	
R	
I	

Session 5	
L	
A	
R	
I	

Session 6	
L	
A	
R	
I	

Session 7

L	
A	
R	
I	

Session 8

L	
A	
R	
I	

and they all had Purpose of Heart...

How To Be Saved

If you have never accepted Jesus Christ as your personal Savior but would like to, read on to find out how to become a Christian.

First, you have to know your condition and the truth about what God says. Romans 3:10, 23 says "There is none righteous, no, not one... For all have sinned and fall short of the glory of God."

Reading one verse further, we see the hope that is in Christ- Romans 3:24: "Being justified freely by His grace through the redemption that is in Christ Jesus."

In John, we see how exactly we can be saved from eternal separation. John 3:16-17: "For God so loved the world, that He gave His only Begotten Son, that whosoever believes in Him should not perish, but have everlasting life. For God did not send His Son into the world to condemn the world, but that the world through Him might be saved."

Jesus came to earth to pay our sin debt in full. He came to save and not condemn, and He paid this price for every single person who has ever lived and who will ever live. That includes YOU! He gave His life for you and loves you more than you could ever fathom. But you have to accept His gift by faith.

Jesus' death and resurrection equalized the playing field for all. By His sacrifice being the price, it doesn't matter if you are rich or poor, have many abilities and resources, or just one. Our works, money, or talents won't get us into heaven, but His precious blood will. Ephesians 2:8-9 confirms this: "For by grace you have been saved through faith, and that not of yourselves; it is the gift of God, not of works, lest anyone should boast."

You can't work your way into heaven; you have to accept His gift by faith!

Faith is a decision, and the actions of your life demonstrate it. Romans 10:9 states, "For with the heart one believes unto righteousness, and with the mouth, confession is made unto salvation."

If you accept His free gift, believe in your heart, and confess with your mouth, you will be saved! If you trust this is true, pray a similar prayer, confessing, repenting, and expressing your faith in Him.

Our God and Father, Thank You so much for giving Your Son to die for my sins. I know I am a sinner and am not right by You because of it. I believe Jesus died for my sins-past, present, and future-and that by accepting His gift, my debt is paid, and I am free in You. I accept His gift and am so thankful for new life. With Your help, I am turning away from sinful habits, and from this day forward, I choose to follow You. In faith, I believe all this to be true because You cannot lie. I love You. In Jesus' Name, Amen!

If you have trusted Jesus for salvation, share your decision with your family, friends, and with me! I'd love to hear from you! If you're not already attending a church, find one for support, community, and growth.

Saved and secure, once and for ALL eternity! John 10:28 "And I give them eternal life, and they shall never perish; neither shall anyone snatch them out of My hand."

Epilogue

I'm not much of a sports person, but I thought about this the other day after something happened in my life. In basketball, there are many different hoop sizes. You can have the colorful "Tiny Tykes" plastic type of hoop up to the standard regulation type of hoop that the professionals play with. God is this standard regulation hoop, and people's standards, or righteousness, and anything not Christ is the "Tiny Tykes" hoop. We can errantly be deceived into thinking our walk with Christ is great because we're making all the "shots" and, of course, "I would never do what they did..." But, can we agree that none of us are righteous and that just because what you or I may do may not be visible to the outside world, we are all sinners saved by grace?

Just like in sports where there's a Hall of Fame, the Bible has one too. The Hall of Faith! Hebrews 11 outlines "Great Heroes of The Faith." I imagine they did not get that commendation by comparing themselves with their peers, practicing comparative righteousness or inaction. I believe they took action and aligned their lives and behaviors with God. While we will never be perfect this side of heaven, we continuously train, practice our "free throws" and aim high with the "regulation hoop". More often than not, we will make the shots, and our scores will improve! We cannot enter into the Hall of Faith if we only play on the Tiny Tykes hoop. We'll never be good enough to play with "the big boys," as they say, and get off the bench because we won't be prepared. His holiness is incomparable to human righteousness. So let's keep practicing with Him as our standard. Let's get off the bench, encourage each other, and be able to say, like Paul, "Follow me as I follow Christ." 1 Corinthians 11:1

... And they all had

Purpose of Heart

Made in the USA
Columbia, SC
06 February 2025